A CLEAR BURNING

A CLEAR BURNING

Poems

NATALIE SAFIR

To order additional copies of this book, contact:
Xlibris Corporation
1-888-795-4274
www.Xlibris.com
Orders@Xlibris.com
23814

CONTENTS

THE HORSES THAT CARRY 13

THE SMOKE FROM THE VILLAGES SHALL CROSS DISTANCES 14

LOVERS 15

STORY OF THE SOUL 16

ROSE DREAMS, LILAC 18

NIGHT LIGHT ALONG THE TRAIL 19

ANIMAL SKIN 20

SOLITUDE 21

WOMAN IN AN ORANGE STRAW HAT 22

WHY COME SO NEAR? 23

WHAT HAS STOPPED? 25

THE OTHER 26

HEART OF THE HIND 27

'NEW FEET WITHIN MY GARDEN GO' 28

THE LONG DAYS 29

BLACKOUT 31

THE CHERRY DAHLIA 33

BREASTS 34

A SINGULAR TREE ARTICULATES FORBEARANCE 36

THE POTS 37

AMARYLLIS 39

REVERE WARE 40

ANNA'S FORK 41

AT MT. HEBRON CEMETERY 42

IN ITS LEAN PRIME 44

THE HERON 45

NOTHING COULD KEEP YOU AWAY 46

MISSING SIMON 47

SEEING 48

LOVE LIKE SNOW 49

SENSIBLE 50

SHIFTINGS 51
COUPLES DAILY 52
RECONCILIATION 53
JOINED TO ITS THICKNESS 54
WAITING FOR THE PERFECT 55
SHADOWING 56
THE YEARS 57
THE INTERVAL 58
HEARTROCK 59
THE CRIMSON 61
THE WORDS FOR WHITE.. 63
SING UP THE WILDFLOWERS 64
GRANDMOTHER OF THE FAITHFUL 65
RED SKY AT NIGHT, EXPLORERS' DELIGHT 66
SNAPSHOTS IN ROME 67
MOON AT PERIGEE 70
DON'T BOTHER ME, MY HEART 71
OUR SPANGLED EARTH 73
THE COLORS OF THE UNIVERSE 74
EAST SIDE BUS STOP 75
SECOND LOOK 76
LIGHTENING THE LOAD 77
AMTRAK FROM NIAGARA FALLS 78
FLESH KNOWS HOME 80
COFFEE AND SYMPATHY 81
HUDSON VALLEY AFTER THE STORM 83
FLYAWAY 84
THE THIRD WOMAN 85
AMPHORA 86
IN THE NIGHT GARDEN 87
FROM THE STANDING AND THE SITTING PLACE 88
SEEDED ROLL 90

ACKNOWLEDGEMENTS

With thanks to the editors of the following journals who have chosen these poems for publication:
THE BERKSHIRE REVIEW: Seeing; THE FLORIDA REVIEW: The Other; HELIOTROPE: Woman in an Orange Straw Hat; The Horses that Carry; HUDSON VALLEY ECHOES: Amaryllis; MID AMERICA POETRY REVIEW: Seeded Roll; MOBIUS; Colors of the Universe; The Years; NATURAL BRIDGE: Breasts; OLD RED KIMONO: Amaryllis; Sing up the Wildflowers; Lightening the Load; PEREGRINE: At Mt. Hebron Cemetery; PIVOT: Lovers; Red Sky at Night, Explorers' Delight; RASKOLNIKOV'S CELLAR: And the Smoke from the Villages; The Cherry Dahlia; RHINO: The Pots; SLANT: The Long Days; SMALL POND MAGAZINE: The Words for White; Hudson Valley After the Storm; SUNSHINE PRESS PUBLICATIONS: Tree Magic, In its Lean Prime.

To my daughters and my grandsons, for Leo, and my student friends
who keep me inspired

"The point is I came back"
from the deep places. Always
there was help, a man or woman
who asked no questions, an animal's
warm body, the itch in my muscles
to climb a swinging rope."

from "Letter from the End of the World"
Lisel Mueller

"What we desire travels with us.
We must breathe time as fishes breathe water."

from "Variations and Reflections on a Theme by Rilke."
Denise Levertov

"And what can you say about one day of life,
a minute, a second: darkness, a light bulb's flash, then dark again?"

from "Return Baggage"
Wislawa Szymborska

THE HORSES THAT CARRY

The horses that carry my sleep come slowly to the tunnel of evening.
Working horses, they drag a dusty wagon behind them
filled with remnants flopping against the slats.
The wooden wheels creak in their turning.

I hear the junkman's call just behind hollow rattles of copper bells.
His musical howl—a long cord of sound—slips through open
and shut windows to find the women waiting to toss out
shirts, trousers dropping to the dusky street.

Then the light slap of worn leather against the horse's flanks, the call
and slow clip-clop disappear around a corner
with the last left scraps of daylight.

My hands release the flat leather straps as we roll into the tunnel,
as the horses continue to pull their load and
the wheels continue their moan.

THE SMOKE FROM THE VILLAGES
SHALL CROSS DISTANCES

You choose it, but it chooses you
the way a young dog bounds toward you
all eagerness, innocence and trust.

He chooses you from the others
(*in Prague, in Budapest and Sofia,
it is tonight*)
because of the way you smell,
what he feels in his fur.

When the red-haired boy leaps over
the back railing to my house
wearing Cossack boots, woolen pantaloons,
a many-colored scarf about his waist,
the fear he stirs within yells out
from my sleep although he has
taken nothing, done nothing
but leap out from the fairytale forest.

He comes because he had to come,
or because secretly in Prague or Sofia
my gypsy blood invited him
to arrive in the night
and not by way of the front door.

LOVERS

belong wherever rope
circles the neck, binds
the waist, anywhere on skin
the burn of friction
might blossom red.

Dangerously they dangle
from outstretched limbs
before a grounded population—
those who slipped the loop,
found refuge in the solitary
wood, those for whom
the rope became its knot.

But the daring, still snared
among the flame trees,
tangle together their scorched
fiber, high at risk
in the electric winds.

STORY OF THE SOUL

I'll be the one who asks
where the soul wanders,
where it lay when I pressed
my lips to her forehead,
warmth still there under the skin.

Was Mother still under her skin
in the place where time stopped.

I'll be the one who tells the story
of her soul flying its way north
to slip through the window
of a granddaughter's dream.

By then the casket and flowers
didn't matter. What mattered
was the long yellow flight,
the college girl curled into the space
behind the face of her elder.

They traveled together through canals,
passages of the inner ear
filled with streaming yolks,
cruising tunnels and curves
sloping toward alliance.

Mother steering, her face
at the prow, her lips describing
to this child of her child
(the whole world was going by)
how to get through it—
with posture of plenitude,
with unbending bone.

ROSE DREAMS, LILAC

Berries on the flowering cherry
vibrate, alarm me.

Tall velour irises flaunt
their yellow lapels.

Peonies flounce foamy shoulders,
and roses repossess their frilly
blossoming fantasies.

Delicate greens crowd into full leaf
as the countryside swells with actuality.

Where is the wind?

Of course late spring frightens me.
Spinning again, remembering nothing
but the long reach of lilac,

I teeter at the edge of flowering,
only to waken dry, this dry desire.

NIGHT LIGHT ALONG THE TRAIL

Under a half moon, we are all the same
age as faces dim in tin light, tree trunks
blacken and stones join shoulders.

The difference between one blue jacket
and a brown coat is only what
memory prompts the eye to recall.

Can we believe grapeberries retain their blues;
do maples drained of reds
only pretend their inky masquerade?

The glow of colors left behind may or
may not reblaze another day
in some other wandering mind.

Surely the heart's turning
from warm to cool
is part of this inconstancy.

ANIMAL SKIN

Just for joy, a dog sails through his skin to meet the ball mid-air.

Spring sends its sure signs and my heart tries to leap fences.

My dog, Tashi, used to return to the house full steam, ears flapping
after happy romps through neighbor's yards, body heat shining.

With pigtails flying, I'd take off down Cortelyou Road on a shiny,
blue bike, or flaunt daring moves on spinning roller wheels.

We chose only newly paved streets to get a speed and smoothness
that slid up our spines as we glided, free, young, joyful.

Once during those years, the shadowy sister that lived within me
pressed fingers hard around the neck of a pesty playmate.
Rage overtook my hands, choking off all reason.

Today, forsythia's in electric frenzy. Gladness inhabits my skin
vigorous as a Saturday afternoon Gene Kelly movie stomping
toward its glossed ending. Back out on the street, blinking
from inside dark, our limitless futures sent us home airborne.

SOLITUDE

all summer you mowed the grass
half awake, half asleep

expecting nothing,
inhaling fragrant silence

after a long time of solitude
the hard prayer
is knowing how to find
the place precise
your shadow becomes
but a richer dimension

crows foretold sustenance
the wind forbid reluctance

all summer you mowed
turning the grass sea smooth

humming, whistling
while eternity moved closer

WOMAN IN AN ORANGE STRAW HAT

after a painting by Pablo Picasso

Look, the shape of her head is not a lie
because it holds the gray face and the green;

the kind eye and the one that cuts glass;
the smiling lip and the lower, trembling half.

Hair springing from one side is golden,
from the other, it falls in colorless sheets.

Who hears her face collapsing into her shoes?

She is looking back a long way
through a landscape of firethorns.

How can she ever be beautiful,
filled with so much hideous dreaming?

WHY COME SO NEAR?

Naked in your firm golden body
you cross the avenue.
The small spindle-legged one
that follows close behind
hesitates at the edge of the road,
flicks her tail and turns as if listening.

You are fragile and light as spring rain.

What brings you so close?
We are full of pride and danger
in our greedy houses, our muscular cars.
We could smash your modest bones,
quiet your graceful song in an instant.

Why come so near?
Behind our abundant grasses,
our patches of sunny daffodils,
destruction is always possible.

It is three in the afternoon.
News of slaughter in Liberia,
sneak bombings in Israel,
nuclear testing in Korea
crowds the radio news.

I feel shame for my breed,
a great longing
to embrace your loveliness.

Move back your boundaries.
Do not come so close to us
and our contaminants.

Flee, enter the woods
with your pure eyes
your slender silent feet.

Everything we have lost is there.

WHAT HAS STOPPED?

The river has lost its wings
and wind, once a feisty pugilist,
cringes behind the hills' skirts.

It is years since the glossy crow
arrested my eyes and old trees
at dawn swayed like elephants.

What stops the natural world
from knocking down my walls,
keeps the stars so far away?

Discouraged dust clutters my place.
Sweaty washcloths stiffen on the rack.

Efforts repeat failure—the needle's
music trapped in one groove.

I did not climb out into the glad
dream I was having.

I did not and he did not and we did not.
I did not and he did not and we.

THE OTHER

Today I am the face behind the face
that floats in its own spittle.
Its old, slimed skin insinuates
into my eyes, rasps my voice box.

What if I set a table for the unwanted?
Serve cakes and chocolates,
feed her until she bloats
into an oil-shined bladder
stretched this as oblivion—
spent devilfish retaining only
a flower of the victim's blood.

But if she continues to fatten,
sucks me with her crushing kiss,
then what force will unclasp
that gummy adherence before
she's made fragrant chum of me?

HEART OF THE HIND

Straight across Broadway
not far from shops, village traffic,
she made the run,
bounding over blacktop to the hedge.

No one will believe she was large
as a fattened pony, her tan hide
a glistening stretch of caramel
lurching through dusk.

I jammed down the brakes—
unthinkable that I might have hit her,
both of us racing to cross
into the next field propelled
by appetite, tensed by fear.

It's the dream that repeats
of running and never being caught,
my legs prancing above pavement.
Whatever pursues me falls away
stunned by my animal courage.

She enters her woodsy haven unscathed.
In the dream it is worth the frantic leaping,
long drafts of terror in mid-air.

'NEW FEET WITHIN MY GARDEN GO'

from a line by Emily Dickinson

One look at the photo of a twelve year-old
posing against the collonade at Prospect Park

and her innermost thoughts become
plain as the buttons on her plaid coat.

New feet within my garden go, yet I pluck
the same wiry brow hairs from that persistent place,

peel the same stubborn hangnail when waiting,
notice my body find its left side in bed.

Moist aroma of river air this evening
repeats to my skin that school is over and

next week I'll begin that thousand piece jigsaw puzzle.

THE LONG DAYS

We'd gobble supper down,
grab a ball and jacks,
a skate-key for 'potsy'
and head for the street.
The boys grouped for 'Ring-o-Levio'
and chose up sides while
the girls squabbled for first.

We roved from one street game
to another as one excited organism
consuming everything in sight.

Some evenings I'd play 47
consecutive games of jacks,
course glibly through "A My Name Is"
enter a double potsy match
and still run down to Silvers'
for a frosty egg cream.

We never imagined becoming adults.
Their world was a remote shadow land
on some hill nobody cared about.
What did it matter if Aunt Ida
was coming to dinner or
Dad had been "let go" again.
So what if they had aches or illnesses,
disappointments or disasters.

The long days in June meant
what I'd heard about menstruation
and how babies got born just wasn't true.
I'd get a boyfriend and
school would never start again.
The War was over for all time
and noone I loved would ever die.

I'm not sure I ever looked
into my mother's face.

BLACKOUT

August nights, after hours
on the cool stone stoop with neighbors
and friends, we took to the fire escapes.
Wet washcloths and fans just weren't enough.

Men stripped to their undershirts,
made silly hats with twisted corners
out of soaked handkerchiefs.

We were hanging in air above the streets;
the brave dangled legs through the bars,
lit and puffed cigarettes without fear
of reprisal or enemy spotters.

We were used to the dark. During the War
our fathers had patrolled the streets
to quash any light seen glowing
from a window or stairwell.

Radio talk seeped from crowded apartments.
Nobody questioned the swollen heat of beds,
how sweat could soak through sheets.
We could stay up here all night if we wanted;
this was the privilege of summer.

In the northeast's blackout tonight
voices outside float in a quiet
free of tv blabber, hum of air conditioners,
microwaves. Traffic, usually
a continuous ocean tide comes to a stop.

You can feel the force of silence.
Crickets madly rub their metallic feet
and stars from the black hole
of the sky glow brighter.

People sit outside in the intimate dark,
waiting for the power to be returned,
the constant thrum of noise and
everything it wipes out.

THE CHERRY DAHLIA

Through rain mist,
the voluptuous, bold face
of the cherry dahlia shines.

One late rose just at bud, twines
toward the porch rail—an infant tongue
at the lip of the step where moisture beads.

Lean stalks appear ready to reinvigorate
and bulge. Rain falls. I am stirred,
expectant as a twenty-year old.

Waking this morning from a lingering dream,
I still see my mother in her red blouse,
the excited roll of her laughter.

Hefty clouds move sedately across the sky.
River gulls weave threads through their density.
An implicit shift resettles the land.

Even as the lusty glow from the one
remaining dahlia persists,
the year's last quarter turns its face away.

BREASTS

I remember with distaste
seeing one of my aunts lift
and dump her full breasts
like potatoes into a sack;
another aunt handling hers
fondly, placing each carefully
into large brassiere cups,
stirred a wistfulness
in me. Mother did it
privately, turning her back
and reappearing to meet my eyes,
intact and covered.

Years later, handling my own
in a matter-of-fact way
after showering, I wonder if
a woman's fondness for them
depends on her man's
appreciation, or absent
a man and children,
do they become only
decorative extras, or
essential sources of comfort?

The pleasure of my own
reminds me of past loves—
nights or mornings
when despite the steel
in my spine or his shoulders,
their plump pillowing
across sheets or under
his fingers, softened
our anger and loneliness.

A SINGULAR TREE ARTICULATES
FORBEARANCE

After a night constricted by silver,
she leans into a sun-patch for release.

Nothing dares move
in the sub-zero vault of air.

Glazed silence unyielding
as a skin of stone.

Around her base, deeply carved
prints, committed to memory.

Glass bound in glinting light,
her disquiet trembles on the sheen.

THE POTS

I'm sorry about the pots.
They came to me stuffed in
a shopping bag, cleaned out first
by one daughter, then the next.
Returned to me for use,
they seemed to belong with
my old kitchen cabinets.

Closing my eyes, I heard
the heavy aluminum clang
to the bottom of the Good Will bin.
You see, I don't have a place
for everything. Your good china's
still unpacked in my cluttered study.

Nor is everything in its place.
And my own pots, leftovers
from marriages, moves, don't have
the gleam and luster of yours
—those sturdy, resolute hands.

When you held mine
as a ten-year old, enjoying
the length of my fingers,
how they differed from your own—
"stubby" you called them,
you pointed me toward the piano,
the easel, the pen.

Wasn't it inevitable those pots
would return to me and
that I would not use them?
I'm sorry. It was your wish.

AMARYLLIS

The plant I brought to enliven
her dying days—she'd call me
with a daily growth report—
the plant I salvaged cleaning out
her apartment stocked with
eight decades of memorabilia,
the last blooms dropped,
stalk soggy from overcare.

Four years I tended the scored stump,
watered, whispered to it.
Then today, not one, but four
red trumpets announced themselves,
rising on a muscular stalk
from the rich soil of heritage.

Blaring from my windowsill
each horn recalls that lively, sturdy woman
daily inching toward me, life size.

REVERE WARE

Mother chastised me
for not scrubbing
the bottoms of pots:
when you take a shower,
don't you wash your backside?
(hint of a chuckle
curled within)

There was no argument.

Look, mom, I'm in mid-life
and doing it, brillo-ing off
twenty years of oxide buildup
from the Reveres, shining up
your loving cup,
the filigree lace platter.

Finally getting it right—
certain things—and I want
your eyes upon me, a nod.

And when uncertainty
envelops me in tarnished grime,
then, most of all, then
let me find your eyes.

ANNA'S FORK

Squares have been filling
with outside dark thick as walls
while I have been reading.

Monumental animals
silent in pitch black paddocks
switch and rustle their tails.

Someone enters under the door
settling down easefully
as a chiffon scarf.

Anna, today by chance,
I found your fork
at a country yard sale,
your name engraved in slender loops,
the sterling's pattern simple
as an olive leaf.

Holding its smooth sides,
I want you to know about
the house I have just bought—
space for a rambling garden,
strong ample trees and
square, forthright rooms
I have entered.

You would be pleased with me.
I have done what you could not.

It's early September and I've still time
to live what you only dreamed.

AT MT. HEBRON CEMETERY

With black umbrellas raised,
we try to hold back
winter's last assault.

We have come here to check
the depth and dimension of stones,
to plan measurements, messages.
We are required to be
definite and precise.

At our feet, the graves of everyone
who raised me, my people, yours.
I stand close to my mother's plot—
a raw tangle of pebbles and dirtballs,
and eye my father's stone.

The distance between them
and me begins to close.
I know I have brought you here
to keep me alive. I place you
between us to alter the balance.

Our hands redden with the sting of cold.
We are still gripping umbrellas when
the snow starts, but we are unprotected.
We turn from the gravesites to each other.

It is the first time you ask me
what I want done when my time comes.
It is the first time you are able to say
Mother, do you want to be here with them?

Daughter, they are mine but I
do not want to join them.
How can I tell you I belong with you.

IN ITS LEAN PRIME

After a night of pounding thunderclaps
a blitz of bolts
from rocky peaks,
I opened my door to find

a tall aspen
uprooted in its lean prime
floating the length
of the blue pool.

I, in my fifties,
sadly noting the fallen tree,
enjoyed the fine line
it cut across water,
how it sectioned the blue
with its spangled limbs.

Across the courtyard
a young man discovering
the stricken tree
inert upon the pool
cried out—

splitting the morning air,
his scream
reached me like fire.

THE HERON

What lies in the heart of the heron
as all night in the shadowed barn
she presses her head into folded wings?

What holds her eyes closed even
when light enters through roof beams
or slants beneath the door?

She may uncurl her neck, glance up
and recoil again. Pleated wings begin to lift,
then crimp, flattening her to floorboards.

Her sky is not planted on solid ground,
her wild grasses might grow if only
they were not watered by salt.

Love sheared her feathers. In dream flight,
she returns to tidelands of home,
illusion scattering as sadness wells up on shore.

Inevitable that she lingers, that hope flies off
the earth. She hobbles with a veteran's uneven gait.
One leg a knobbed stilt, the other a broken sail.

NOTHING COULD KEEP YOU AWAY

Days you sang and danced for your hero,
dazzled him with oriental scarves, nougats
from Italy, the last bars of an old melody.

Nights, thick ropes that bound you
to each other began to unravel.
A network of tubes over his hospital bed
obscures your face. He is yielding
the long story of his bones to the shadows.
You walk the corridors desperate for a map.

You offer him your golden voice,
weather reports from tropical shores,
oranges from China, but only
the last two lines of your song remain.
He smiles. By dawn, what's left of
your broken song does not reach him.

Late this afternoon in the long rays
of October at the corner of my garden,
a monarch butterfly, large as a finch
sucks greedily at the nectar of a bright bloom.

And if he dies while sucking, I believe
all the sweetness that has filled his body,
will lift and carry him up.

MISSING SIMON

Grief is a fire of pain
through the flesh,
my friend cries

staring as
the toaster's coil
of hot wires turns

from curly orange
to thinner and thinner
threads of kohl.

I watched my husband's
body dwindle
like that, she sighs,

burrowing deeper
into his sweater,
his trousers
hanging limp
over her lank hips.

I've heard of widows
who cake mud
all over their bodies,

and one who tattooed
her lost beloved's
name
on every inch
of her stinging flesh.

SEEING

after the Pierre Bonnard exhibit

You see the figure and face emerge from the corner,
unexpected, unsought, peeking around table and window.

A figure that you passed and repassed while fixed
elsewhere, finds its way toward you, so you
wonder was it there before it slid into foreground.

Ask yourself how it was possible not to notice that face,
even when the tangled landscape, the patterned
wallpaper and colored blocks of tile dazzled.

The eyes you brought were not seeing all the way to
their edges, eyes you brought were seduced by reds,
easily fell into the orange path glowing like glass.

Can you excuse eyes that could not
see more than what was then visible?

LOVE LIKE SNOW

Love clumps like snow on
boughs quite high. The small
flakes fall and bits of them
through wind and air, drop down
to crotch of limbs, to bark
once black and bare.

You walk, you sniff white sky,
chill air, and as you walk
from where you are to where
you go, the crunch of it
on step and stone lifts part
of you that's not alone.

But love like snow in shine
or storm, can turn to ice.
Take form in fear of what we're
not. Stack up dirt black, pile hard
as rage—each mound that's left
at curb or ledge, some stage of rot.

Still ground or wind blown wild,
it coats the eye and bends the will.
Its fret-work mild, its heart pure glass,
by spring the ghost of it has passed.

SENSIBLE

full puffy snow
finally came
she had nothing to do with it
couldn't even see it
though it soaked
through her boots

a chore like any other—
windshields to broom off
a footpath to forge

as if she cared if it never
snowed again, as if
she believed that spray
that sparkle
could ever

thrill her again
send her reeling
out into
the marvel of it

better not to think about love
or wildness,
better
to stay sensible, old,
clean off boots, scowl

grumble like
everybody else

SHIFTINGS

The day the season shifts—
outside a sudden bloomingness startles
and baby smooth air slides over skin.

Winter's shaved profile puckers,
stubbly with fuzz,
crinkly with growth.

You look up to find night
covering over seams
with a fine leather glove.

Distance and difference have run
off to hide in her fingertips.

COUPLES DAILY

Get up, old man! the woman
said, I don't like getting old.
Okay, he sighed. They boiled eggs,
had a walk, read the paper,
talked, did supper,
watched a film. It was dark.

Don't go to bed! she said.
No? There's still tomorrow,
he said. But, she moaned,
tomorrow it's all over again.

She made him sit eyes open
in a chair and count each minute.
Tick tock, it's all going by, she said.
Let's sit here until we're dead.

Oh, but I'm bored, he groaned.
You're not alone, she said.
I won't be left, he said, behind.
I'll get there first if you don't mind.

Don't mind if you do, she said,
for years you've worked at
being ahead, in this last race,
I won't be far behind.

RECONCILIATION

Her one good eye strains, carrying its usual burden
of optimism, romance. The left, a visceral wound
whose corner houses a charcoal cloud, tunnels inward

to what she cannot deny—what's ugly in the world;
the beast part of those she loved, fragments that
don't cohere, but roar, spit and strike to leave a mark.

The tender eye lives in dust motes sprinkling morning,
in yellow curtains soaked with early sun and in

the clear crescent high at dusk—but compromised,
aware of a disillusioned partner locked on merciless fact.

JOINED TO ITS THICKNESS

It does not wash off like watercolor.
Does not steam or soap off
like the penny decals we stuck
on our arms to pretty them up.

Doesn't peel like potato skins
to reveal surprising eyes.
Or pick off—a scab releasing
dead cells into bathwater.

If peeled at all, it smarts the way
a hot-waxed layer parts from the skin,
underlayers stained with color—
fresco of blood, lymph
and mortar wed to the fascia.

So soaked down, the horizontal scrape
of fingernails encounters there
another layer beneath the last,
and another, steeped in hues
joined to its thickness.

>   *And if I could, would it even matter, since*
>   *my heart prefers its dumb grieving to the real.*

WAITING FOR THE PERFECT

My graceful one, missing two years, or
an amazing likeness, was seen at day's end.
I come seeking a lost cat who may not want to be found.
A drench of rain hangs; a swarm of gnats circles.

I'm told she crossed the path, looked
toward her home, paused in a moment
of disdain or longing, then
disappeared into the woods below.

How can I be here at the appointed hour waiting,
and how not? How can the girl I was be real
as the call of wood thrush,
swish of squirrel tails against the leaves?

Childish questions—such as what is love—
old answers that might have been true,
now speckled lizards that curl around
the fifth chamber of my heart.

Clarity—perfect cat, vibrant poem, lost
just before weeks of battering rains.

From the edge of the bench, restless and
vexed by my naivete, I watch and fidget.

The perfect poem waits near the base of
some tree for a signal I have not mastered.

SHADOWING

If as ritual, you watch every sunset over the river, eyes
west even on rainy days, you learn about faith and truth,
where you've been and the likelihood of tomorrow.

If you practice gathering droplets of dew just before dawn,
scooping drops from stem, blade and leaf to a glass siphon,
you learn about patience and transformation.

At noon, there's nothing to do but look straight up or down,
wait for the miniscule motions that will soon shadow-mark
the exact place where you stand—the way Chinese calligraphy

edges and fills rice paper, blotting into the white, both
of the surface and on it, arriving in its own
but dependent shape to extend and deepen form.

Just as I follow and record this shadow side emanating
daily from my body induced by every swing of light,
walking attached to its opposite, twinned at the source.

THE YEARS

Sea water's rolling in so fast, each time we move our chairs,
shoes, towels, books back and get comfortable,

the tide's already at our feet, aluminum chair legs sinking
into glistening undertow, reading matter in danger.

When your shoes almost floated away, we drew back
fifteen or so feet, confident we could keep well ahead.

I turned around to look back—stretched, smoothed and
silkened, the moist sand had been cleared of wrinkles.

Children nearby build castles, stout turrets, an embalmed wall,
the moat dug deep as little shovels can go.

As the trough fills, walls crumble, a large crack
in the fundament begins the slow toppling.

The last to succumb is a glossy pebble adorning the parapet.
From the tower window, still fluttering, a white feather.

THE INTERVAL

Long-legged swan bird slides into
water ribbons curling around her.

She's an empress of evening
jeweled with memories.

Shades of remorse
shadow her wingtips.

She's a hand stroke
across the body of a cello,
prow of music at the marsh edge.

The snowmoon's smile
rises within a furred halo.

How quickly if we do not catch it
the sparkling moment is gone.

The white bird flaps
and finds land.

Her call is a brown note of warmth
beyond sadness, beyond bare trees.

The interval between my
voice and hers closes.

The moon slips down to touch blades
of grass, tell the stones they are immortal.

HEARTROCK

The sinewy heart-like rock
glowing underwater
in the low tidal lace
of the Cape shore
we walked days after
our wedding, now

hardens into a fist
on the tray with other
sea-smoothed stones
we carried home.

It has returned to gray,
bulge of chambers fixed—
the way lips,
after fifty years,
prepare then
fit their attitude.

I turn the bulk
of the rough valentine
in my hand, hold
its dead heft and wonder
at its coincidence
with the living thing.

As if snatched
by forceps quickly
from the warm corpse,
this heart retains
an imprint
of a life before—

our footprints entering,
leaving the tidal shore.

THE CRIMSON

I had been thinking about deer,
how they disappear into the woods
soundlessly, only crescents
in snow left behind, when

flattened out, the pelt of a squirrel
still holding its shape on blacktop
lay before me—rear legs curled under
fur fresh and vibrant in sun,

but its tail was tipped by crimson,
as if in the head's crushing
the flick of it lightly brushed
the walnut skull
opened up on the driveway.

This one, not a baby and
not quite quick enough,
or a brief hesitation,
a misjudgment held him
as tires ironed him solid.

A moment of still breathing,
can cost life's continued flow.
How often poised
on the rim of not knowing,
I dart out unsure of
the attraction or pause there
unwilling to find out.

They can turn back
midway across the road
calculating to a hair the speed
and size of what's approaching.

Was his eye caught
by blackbirds gathering
in the gnarled magnolia,
a cat nearby on the prowl or
a memory of last month's treasures
buried before the high snows?

This morning's warming sun
won't preserve his splayed body
but moves along the rotting
I carefully bypass—
all the while eyeing that crimson.

THE WORDS FOR WHITE

You read the ground for tracks,
sniff the air for grouse,
watchful for a rustle in the bush,

then ask for a vocabulary of snow,
fresh words for the comfort of silence,
the lengthening shawl that unfolds the land.

My eyes search the enchantment
of a white sky for signs—

a way to shape letters
from the fog of my breath.

Snow, I begin to see, has been
love for me through many winters.

In the drift of flakes, from the light
they hold, words are supplanted
by tall man, long branch, brown dog

falling

lightly

SING UP THE WILDFLOWERS

When by chance you meet someone
with strong hands, eyes wide apart
both level and merry, who looks at you
with appetite, happy to discern
just what's wonderful about you—

it's like stumbling upon a patch of monarda
rolling over a field that you already love.
Without cultivation, strain or plan, the gift
appears, fully realized, glorious in half-sun.

Their loveliness opens in you.
To gather them up in hand or skirt
would be a travesty of sorts.

To pluck them would truncate the very heart
of serendipity, pinch off discovery
for another wandering hopefully.

GRANDMOTHER OF THE FAITHFUL

Now I am wolf, grandmother of the faithful,
jaw raised to the moon's fullness.

My cubs tumbling on the ledge hunt for themselves.
In our littered den where my mate drowses,
each fresh wind stirs me to the prowl.

Tawny fur clumps my haunches.
The pressure of years pushes me toward
the straightest path my nostrils can discern.

In winter light, by the wide river, my hopes light fires.

Wise and fierce, cap glowing with night sky embers,
an attendant raven travels on my outskirts
bearing messages from the sapphire void.

His eyebeams slice through fog; his curved beak
is a scythe to cut cloud, pierce the prey
reeling in his raptor brain.

Propelled by a lean winter toward sustenance, we
are a wary alliance traveling the rim of affliction.

RED SKY AT NIGHT, EXPLORERS' DELIGHT

Excited by the rosy sky surrounding Mars,
scientists begin the search for life
in its rock formations, send the toy truck, Rover
to wobble and snoop into crevices, cracks
where dust and basalt of stars,
a red slime bubbles.

Already it smacks of Disney.

See the vermilion beads aggregating,
percolating in energetic samba
between stones in ooze pools.
Adorable, amusing, it's art!

More life and what to do with it,
while in a greed-frenzy we exploit,
expend, violate, take for granted
bulb flicks of the firefly,
comic ingenuity of the chipmunk,
grenade-like cones of spruce,
every startling sunset.

Up there, mindful of the commercial
possibilities, Mickey Mouse polka dots
dance about in a life jig
hell bent on entertaining us.

SNAPSHOTS IN ROME

Bubbling fountains of words
tumble from lips, laughter
splashes out in spurts,
charged dialogue bouncing
up and back through
Campo Dei Fiori.
Mouths, tongues, palates. Appetite.
                    *

Black draped, an ancient, bent nun
no taller than an eight-year-old
stumbles along with cane and beggar's basket
between tourists on *Via Condotti*
drunk with shopping.
                    *

Each time I throw down a cigarette butt
to the cobblestones in the square,
I think of the women
in neon cover-ups cleaning the streets
every morning with straw brooms
straggly as old men's beards.
Each woman is trailed by
a bundled-up toddler making circles
around mama as she sweeps.
Tight circles it will be hard to step across.
                    *

A lack of nerve keeps me silent
about the grandiose, brutal
remains of the Coliseum.
          *

From the train to *Ostia Antica*
each person in a person's place.
Each person's place atop the next.
So many lives, so many days.
Oggi. Each living each life.
          *

The old man and his prized Willy
come daily together to the square.
When I ask to take their picture
his face beams and he summons Willy
but the small dog runs off to pee
on the cornerstone of the French Embassy.
He laughs, relishes Willy's testiness,
calls him again and again.
          *

From the piazza on Trastevere's highest hill,
Rome spreads out its colorful mosaic
to mountains where Orvieto, Spoleto lie sleeping.

Why would I miss buildings that scrape the sky
when it is better left to itself?
          *

In the dream my hair is dark and wavy.
Its luxuriant fur rests over my shoulders.
He is talking to me, but when I begin to answer
he has begun looking somewhere else.
          *

I retouch the thirty-year dream I have carried
of the grace of the *Campidoglio*.
Lithe marble youths beside restless muscled horses.
                    *

Older, well-heeled Romans, without
opening their mouths, are unmistakable.

The toothless vendor in Campo Dei Fiori
sells us the sweetest *mandarini*,
juiciest oranges, tastiest bananas.

I wake from my nap uttering *pomeriggio, pomeriggio*
over and over as if it belonged to me.

MOON AT PERIGEE

Nothing prepared me for the indelible fire
high in the black night sky; nothing
prepared me for that circle blazing

full-faced from the east, undiminished
by the velvet dark, its presence
deepening dimension there.

The searchlight stare turned full on me.
A clear burning, uncomfortably near
my pin-point of winter ground.

Willing specimen before its cutting glare,
targeted, my small life in telescopic scrutiny
fixed to the planet, finite, ordinary.

The dwarf of me hunched under covers
to shrink epiphany to common size,
reach what wisdom solitude might teach.

Yet even out of sight, that eternal soloist
reflects back one-ness—each examined
life forever pinned within its sphere.

DON'T BOTHER ME, MY HEART

Cat staring out the window;
leaves spun by invisible whips.

Aroma of ripe bananas;
small gnats gather from nowhere.

A dark ribbed sweater, a car door slams.
Her brush tip tail begins to scheme.

Slippered feet approaching,
sky flying away on reddening carpets.

One orange pillow goes into hibernation;
the message never reaches its destination.

What is the texture of desire?
Drying petals in a cracked ceramic jug.

A friend from high school tells me even then
I loved Baudelaire. I knew then what I know.

Don't bother me about love, my heart.
Retreat into the quiet space that leaves cover.

Don't call him *mon mari*. Call him otherwise,
a noun of significance but quite imprecise.

Clog at curbside. Wilder winds, some steadily
dropping rain is called for.

Sewer drainage has to reach the river basin;
you must stop listening to Piaf or

embracez le douleur like a friend just returned
from a failed trip who may never travel again.

OUR SPANGLED EARTH

More cherished now, our spangled earth
sends up astonishing beauty,
an urgent pleasure bordering on pain.

The leaves hold on as we do—
tarnished, older, carrying wounds
of our late summer grief.
In pleated skirts, they flame
against a childish blue sky,
a sustained, dazzling light
challenging my sorrow—
bright young faces of the dead,
their severed lives squandered
in the name of one god or another.

Hasn't there been enough destruction
to satisfy the bitter god of ashes.

What can we offer the angels of mercy?

THE COLORS OF THE UNIVERSE

Astonomers spoke too soon;the universe isn't turquoise.

Now we are expected to accept our world as the beige
of office furniture, computers, file cabinets,
factual, undressed and absent expression.

Eons of poets were mistaken—celestrial blue was
only the pigment of imagination.
Have all tones smashed into drone faced beige?

How much more we loved our spinning globe
when it was blue, its waters brimming with sky's gift.

Tenderness welled up in us, devotional sighs,
murmurs of everlasting prettiness, faith that our story
on the planet had a chance to come out right.

EAST SIDE BUS STOP

You can tell the ones fleeing,
the sidewalk pursuing them.
A woman with the brisk bearing
of a marine sergeant
is gaining on her goals.

You can tell the ones
who want to be elsewhere
and those so caught
they fail to feel the air
twirling fans of the gingkos.

On board, the large man
blocking the rear door
is a puffing bull
straddling his space.
The girl in the next seat
distresses her cracked fingers.

Fear empties the eyes
of the well-dressed woman
hesitant to place her foot
on the exit step.

The song of the contented
reaches you too, though
their eyes will not meet yours.
Wary as kids licking ice-cream
cones among the hungry,
they covet the cream,
brace against any lurch
that could hurl it downward.

SECOND LOOK

The daffodils are yellower
than any idea of yellow

painted beside the curving lawn
where two cherry trees drop
snowcups onto the breeze.

Shiny grackles hop among the stalks.

The bee hesitates
above every daffodil—
each opening a small dazzling sun

until he finds
the tulip's buttery mouth
and melts within.

Fat grackles hop about the stalks
stealing bits of canvas.

LIGHTENING THE LOAD

When Del decides to move
he builds a bonfire—a great
orange blossom in the backyard
that eats love letters, books, clothes,
everything he no longer needs.
As cinders cool, he just leaves.

Emily faces a wall. Rising
before her, accumulations
in stacks pen her in.
It's all around me, she sighs,
unable to even think
how to knock it all down.

Nikki thinks she'd like to split.
But if she discards even one piece,
the whole construct of cards
would collapse with such a whoosh,
she'd be blown right out the door.
She dare not touch a thing.

Talia keeps moving, lugging
possessions on her back,
depositing the old in a new place.
She's a land tortoise changing
the terrain so that what's still
with her appears different.
Nothing's lighter, only more transparent.

AMTRAK FROM NIAGARA FALLS

On the long morning train, an intimacy
that began the night before,
sleeps soundly between couples.

A woman clasps her man's shoulder
like a blanket; the rapid slide
of trees is their boudoir curtain.

Another stares blindly at mountains
going by from here to there, while
for years her partner reads the newspaper.

Breathing heavily across adjacent seats,
the college boy, strewn among belongings,
curls up in twisting layers of thought.

Babies, boneless in sleep, call out surprising notes.
One cry turns to a chuckle as mother,
moving routinely, does her job into morning.

Other trains flank us, flash by rushing forward
with urgent unanswered questions
and out along the windy river, where?

Through a night of turns, wedge-cuts through rock,
we've become a disheveled, settled family.
Eyes burrow, blink as we tunnel into Manhattan.

Aisles come to the end of a long winding sentence
that breaks into stutters, then mono-syllabic
jolts. Lap-tops close, newspapers fold.

Doors slide open onto a thick concrete platform.
Once on our feet, we escalate up into the huge
gathering place. We merge, become other outsiders.

FLESH KNOWS HOME

Flesh knows the feel of home,
a plumped comfort both rises and
settles to the skin. Long tunnels
built by generational brick line
the throat, far sights from hilltops
lie over backdrops of tender blue.

Flesh knows there are few true homes
where cellars hoard anonymous secrets,
footsteps imprint the hallway, fear floods
the basement, laughter rolling above
word games whose complex syntax
remains known only to one or two.

Flesh knows home has its colorful
recurring pleasures like painted dreams,
a story only one person can tell,
pictures roiling on a private screen,
bomb scares and constructed shelters,
an aging mirror outside and within.

On the road map that wanders up and
down the coast, one moving destination
is carried in a locket engraved with N,
a hidden ring still gleams in its box.
Flesh feels the pull of its heavy hand,
the far cry always arriving at the next bend.

COFFEE AND SYMPATHY

A robust fuzzy fly
somehow fell into the remains
of my evening coffee.
I heard him flailing there,
legs sputtering and spinning
in futile locomotion.

Earlier he'd sailed through my rooms
with buzzing bravado
dive-bombing me and
my wide-eyed tabby.
We wanted to swat him.

But I've been stuck
many times in the wrong broth
when some hand reached
out to set me right.

His crumbly body itched
at my conscience.

I angled the cup on its side,
drained the liquid
to give him an even chance.

Working his wiggly legs
up the slippery side
then fluffing himself even faster
than my sympathy evaporated,
he was up and out
and didn't look back.

Noisy fanfare above my head.
The higher he soared, the more I hated him.

HUDSON VALLEY AFTER THE STORM

Shape this phrase to the curve of branches
raised from tree trunks to the washed sky.

Guide the eye to branch tips that arrow-mark
blurred air. Cross an expanse of tinted space

with clear bird strokes; dab smoky green
onto far hills, backed by timber browns.

Leave the long, monotone river that crosses,
to lie in its muddied confusion.

Where the scene stops, leave the white page white.

FLYAWAY

Seed flakes—
unlikely messengers
from a deeply troubled sky—ping
the pavement, bounce about.
Trees are not eager for this tympany.

When sky turns solid, and the flurry
flowers, a young pregnant woman
smiles inwardly. Car hoods and
sidewalks cover with fleece.

Just a taste for the tip of the tongue.
Soon bright blue fields above and
like a quick kiss that never happened,
clouds run away, a glisten

left on the land.

THE THIRD WOMAN

Two curvaceous figures draped
in delectable pink flesh recline
while the third woman, loosely
clothed in green sits behind them.

We have been skillfully drawn:
one is a bold assumption, another
a vivid implication, and the third
is essential to the composition.

My counterparts and I are
posed in precarious balance.
Within this scene a struggle
for position is developing.

If the third woman stands up
and leaves the picture, the aesthetic
demands that the other two
also rise up and go home.

AMPHORA

With hands on her hips, she's aware of the softening—
arms growing loopy and smooth, hips plumping out to contour
of plum and orange, the space between her thighs disappearing.

Before her head lolls off never to be useful again,
she stares down at both feet melding into a wide base
planted on a sunny terrace overlooking the Aegean.

Rotund, she's become housing for a dark mix of aging wine.
Volumes of it rise, fill her from side to side—old loves,
sweet sorrows and bitter tears soak her walls in hearty distillation.

Fine physiques of fleet young men dance, carrying shields and
swords around her circumference, skillfully mount chariots
etched with proud insignias of wars won and enemies slain.

At festivals or grand symposia, they'll tip her forward to pour
forth the mix or penetrate her aromatic interior and imbibe,
those curvaceous sides both container and source of the solution.

IN THE NIGHT GARDEN

Spider mums stand tall through dark,
listening with their hidden eastern eyes
from a clearwater jar.
Speechless, white-wrapped warriors,
they hear my dream life, guard
as at a smoked glass door,
the flighty creatures of my nights,
hold them still in moving focus
so when morning light spreads
out the physical nature
of my room, figures
still sting, scrape, or cling
to my skin.

Lean white sentinels
of concentration
protect the mysteries,
the fragile revelations.

FROM THE STANDING AND THE SITTING PLACE

Cats tell us what we need to hear.
I listen to the message of the old one
stretching her eighteen years

like a peaceful river across
the mahogany table. She eyes the door,
all day watching, lifting only her head.

And the brave scamp, Clarity, who has lived
in the wild, pads closer when the doctor
arrives with the white needle.

She places herself beneath the glass table,
legs folded under—a small sphinx
focused on the drama.

Lilli, the youngest, frets vocally at the top
of the stairs. Afterwards, when the body
has been taken, her sniffing and mewing

linger into the night. She cries out for
comfort, reassurance—poor
substitute for an infusion of courage.

Cowardly lioness, haunted by wondering
wanders for days through the scent
of the elder's disappearance, while

her feisty sibling, toughened
by witnessing, grooms herself,
curls comfortably within her strength.

It is a triad of stages, I think. All of them mine.

SEEDED ROLL

I sit down with a four-inch
fat folder of old letters,
his and mine,
plow my way through.
My god, I *did* know
what I thought
I didn't at the time.
And I had to have it,
even if it wasn't
what I really wanted.

At Bela's, I order a seeded roll.
The guy at the counter says:
If we don't have it,
you want it anyway?
Sure, I say, sure.
Of course I do.

NATALIE SAFIR has been publishing poems in literary journals since the 1970's and her work has been anthologized in several college texts. Her earlier books are Moving into Seasons, To Face the Inscription, and Made Visible about which poet Thomas Lux wrote: "I admire very much these utterly lucid, distilled, and powerful poems."

She was a founding editor of Gravida, poetry editor of Inprint, and founder/director of the Pomegranate Reading Series. She continues to teach poetry and creative writing in her community and developed a unique approach to Writing as Healing that combines her skills as poet and Gestalt Therapist.